Fly Away Owl!

by Ronda Greenberg

illustrated by Chad Thompson

Scott Foresman
is an imprint of

PEARSON

Glenview, Illinois • Boston, Massachusetts • Chandler, Arizona
Upper Saddle River, New Jersey

ISBN 13: 978-0-328-50792-4
ISBN 10:   0-328-50792-X

9 10 V010 15 14 13

One day a boy was playing in his yard. He saw something near a pile of wood. It was an owl. The owl was hurt.

The boy yelled for his dad. His dad opened the door and came out.

His dad looked at the owl. Then he called an animal shelter. That's a place where you can take hurt animals.

A woman from the shelter came and looked at the owl. Its wing was broken.

The woman knew what to do. She put the owl in a cage and took it back to the shelter.

The woman made sure the owl was resting and warm. She fixed its wing.

It was time to feed the owl. The woman gave the owl mice. Owls like mice.

Many weeks passed. Finally the
owl could fly. His wing was better. He
should go back into the wild.

The woman called the boy who found
the owl. It was time to let the owl go.

The boy and his dad went to meet the woman near a forest.

"Time to fly away," said the woman.

The boy loved watching the owl fly high. They all waved. "Good-bye," they shouted.